For the Teacher

This reproducible study guide consists of lessons to use in conjunction with a specific novel. Used together, the books and the guide provide an exciting supplement to the basal reader in your classroom. Written in chapter-by-chapter format, the guide contains a synopsis, pre-reading activities, vocabulary and comprehension exercises, as well as extension activities to be used as follow-up to the novel.

In a homogeneous classroom, whole class instruction with one title is appropriate. In a heterogeneous classroom, reading groups should be formed: each group works on a different novel on its reading level. Depending upon the length of time devoted to reading in the classroom, each novel, with its guide and accompanying lessons, may be completed in three to six weeks.

Begin using NOVEL-TIES for reading development by distributing the novel and a folder to each child. Distribute duplicated pages of the study guide for students to place in their folders. After examining the cover and glancing through the book, students can participate in several pre-reading activities. Vocabulary questions should be considered prior to reading a chapter; all other work should be done after the chapter has been read. Comprehension questions can be answered orally or in writing. The classroom teacher should determine the amount of work to be assigned, always keeping in mind that readers must be nurtured and that the ultimate goal is encouraging students' love of reading.

The benefits of using NOVEL-TIES are numerous. Students read good literature in the original, rather than in abridged or edited form. The good reading habits, formed by practice in focusing on interpretive comprehension and literary techniques, will be transferred to the books students read independently. Passive readers become active, avid readers.

Novel-Ties are printed on recycled paper.

SYNOPSIS

Sam and Rosa are a middle-aged couple who maintain an on-shore lighthouse. Although childless, they are never lonely for they have befriended a hundred sea gulls who fly to the lighthouse every day for food and a place to land. The kindly couple have even given names to the gulls that they avidly paint and photograph.

One night a savage storm lashes the lighthouse. After surveying the damage, Sam and Rosa realize they cannot rebuild the structure. They sadly pack their belongings and move inland to a small house far from the sea.

The couple likes their new house and their neighbors, but they miss the sea gulls. To encourage the birds to come for a visit, Sam and Rosa shine a big light from the roof of their new suburban home.

Before very long, the sea gulls arrive. Sam and Rosa introduce the sea gulls to their new neighbors, and everyone enjoys feeding the birds. After a while, Sam and Rosa's "lighthouse children" fly away, for sea gulls cannot stay in one place very long. The couple, however, keeps their bright light shining to make sure the gulls will return.

PRE-READING ACTIVITIES

1. Look at the cover of *The Lighthouse Children* and read the title. What do you think the book will be about? Who might be the lighthouse children? Do you know the author's name? Have you read any other books by him?

2. Find some pictures of lighthouses. Bring them into class.

3. Have you ever seen a real lighthouse? Did you go inside? Tell what you know about lighthouses. What important jobs do lighthouses do?

4. Can you think of a time when you

   - fed some birds or other wild animals?
   - lived through a bad thunderstorm?
   - moved to a new neighborhood and missed your friends?
   - lost a pet and then found it again?

   Tell a friend about one of these experiences. Then write about what happened.

5. Do you have any pets? Do your friends have pets? List three reasons why you think people like to keep pets.

   1. _____

      _____

   2. _____

      _____

   3. _____

      _____

Pre-Reading Activities (cont.)

6. Think of a time when you had a good idea about how to solve a problem. Write about it in the story frame below.

The problem I faced was _____

_____

_____. In order to

solve it, I decided to _____

_____

_____. My idea worked because

_____

_____.

PAGES 5 - 11 [HarperTrophy "An I Can Read Book"]

Vocabulary: Read the words in the Word Box. Then write each word next to its clue. The letters in the boxes spell something this story is about.

WORD BOX

| lighthouse | couple | shone | beam |
| lonely | guide | hungry | careful |

---

1. gave off light   ☐ __ __ __ __

2. taking care not to get hurt   __ __ __ ☐ __ __ __

3. ray of light   __ __ ☐ __

4. wanting to eat food   __ __ __ ☐ __ __

5. show the way   __ ☐ __ __ __

6. two people together   __ __ __ __ ☐ __

7. feeling sad about being alone   ☐ __ __ __ __ __

8. tower with a bright light   __ __ __ __ __ __ __ __ ☐ __

Answer: __ __ __   __ __ __ __ __

Read to find out why Sam and Rosa are never lonely.

Story Questions:

1. How do lighthouses help ships?

2. Why aren't Sam and Rosa ever lonely?

3. Why do the sea gulls fly to the lighthouse?

Pages 5 - 11 (cont.)

4. How do you know that Sam and Rosa like the sea gulls?

5. Why do the sea gulls fly away from the lighthouse?

Picture Questions:

1. How do you know that Sam and Rosa are old?

2. What do Sam and Rosa feed the gulls?

3. How do Sam and Rosa carry food to the gulls?

Rhyming Names:

Sam and Rosa gave the sea gulls names that rhyme — Ernie and Bernie, Dora and Cora, Molly and Dolly, Lanny and Nanny, Helga and Zelga. See if you can name some more of the birds. List as many rhyming pairs as you can.

_____ and _____

_____ and _____

_____ and _____

Compound Words:

The word *lighthouse* is made up of two words — *light* and *house*. Draw a line from each word on the left to a word on the right to make a compound word. Write the compound words on the lines.

1. cook   a. horn   _____

2. fog   b. place   _____

3. house   c. out   _____

4. fire   d. work   _____

5. home   e. boat   _____

Pages 5 - 11 (cont.)

Science Connection:

Keep a list of some different types of birds you see this week. Choose the one you like most. Draw a picture of it and write a few sentences about it. See if you can find a book that tells more about this bird.

Art / Writing Activity:

Pretend you are one of the sea gulls in the story. Tell why you like to fly to the lighthouse. Then tell about another place you like to go. Draw a picture to show this place.

PAGES 12 - 17

Vocabulary: Use the words in the Word Box and the clues below to fill in the puzzles.

> *WORD BOX*
>
> worry   tomorrow   foghorn   storm   damage   crashed

1. strong wind with heavy rain

2. horn to guide ships

3. harm or hurt something

4. hit hard with a loud noise

5. feel uneasy

6. day after today

Now use the words in the Word Box to fill in the blanks in the sentences below.

1. The ship heard the _____ and sailed away from the rocks.

2. The dark clouds make me think it will rain _____.

3. The _____ was so bad our roof blew off.

4. If you hold the railing, you do not have to _____ about falling.

5. The car slid on the ice and _____ into a truck.

6. Did the fire do any _____ to your kitchen?

Pages 12 - 17 (cont.)

> Read to find out what happens to the lighthouse.

Story Questions:

1. Why don't Sam and Rosa worry when the sea gulls fly away?

2. How do Sam and Rosa keep ships safe?

3. What happens to the lighthouse during the storm?

4. What do Sam and Rosa decide to do after the storm?

Picture Questions:

1. What makes the light in the lighthouse tower?

2. What shows that it is a bad storm?

3. What happens to the lighthouse door?

Math Connection:

Imagine these are the 100 sea gulls that visit Sam and Rosa.

}}}}}}}}}}}}}}}}}}}}}}}}}
}}}}}}}}}}}}}}}}}}}}}}}}}
}}}}}}}}}}}}}}}}}}}}}}}}}
}}}}}}}}}}}}}}}}}}}}}}}}}

How many sea gulls are in each row? _____

How many groups of 4 are in 100? Count them off. _____

Suppose only half the gulls came. How many is that? _____

Art / Writing Activity:

Suppose everyone got together and built a new lighthouse for Sam and Rosa. What colors would it be? Would it have to be round? Draw a picture of a building. Then tell why you think it would make a good lighthouse.

PAGES 18 - 25

Vocabulary: Draw a line from each word on the left to its meaning on the right. Then use the numbered words to fill in the blanks in the sentences below.

1. visit   a. people who live nearby

2. edge   b. not fancy, simple

3. waited   c. stayed in one place to see something happen

4. cookouts   d. place where something begins

5. neighbors   e. go or come to see someone

6. plain   f. meals cooked and eaten outside

. . . .

1. We _____ all day, but our friends never came.

2. I served a(n) _____ cake because I had no time to make an icing.

3. I hope our new _____ will have a child my age.

4. If you live at the _____ of a forest, you can expect to have deer in your yard.

5. Many people serve hot dogs and hamburgers at _____.

6. We always _____ our grandparents on holidays.

Read to find out about Sam and Rosa's new house.

Story Questions:

1. Where do Sam and Rosa move?

2. Why aren't Sam and Rosa ever lonely in their new house?

Pages 18 - 25 (cont.)

3. What do Rosa and Sam miss about living at the lighthouse?

4. Why don't the birds come to visit Sam and Rosa?

5. What do Sam and Rosa do to tell the sea gulls where they live? Do you think their plan will work?

Picture Questions:

1. How do Sam and Rosa travel to their new home?

2. What food do the neighbors serve at the cookout?

3. How do Sam and Rosa decorate their house?

Questions for Discussion:

1. Have you ever moved to a new neighborhood? What are some good ways to get to know your new neighbors?

2. If you had to move away from your house and school, what do you think you would miss the most?

Science Connection:

In Salt Lake City, Utah, there is a big statue of a sea gull. Long ago, insects were about to eat all the farmers' crops. Just in time, sea gulls flew in and ate up the insects. The people were so happy they built the statue. Think of other animals that help people. Draw a picture of one of these animal helpers. Then write a sentence telling how it helps.

Art / Writing Activity:

Make believe you are a sea gull in the story. Tell what you are doing now that Sam and Rosa are not at the lighthouse. Tell what it is like to fly and why gulls "can't stay in one place for very long." If you like, draw a gull's-eye-view of your neighborhood from the sky.

Pages 18 - 25 (cont.)

Literary Element: Setting

Fill in the chart to compare Sam and Rosa's lighthouse with their new home.

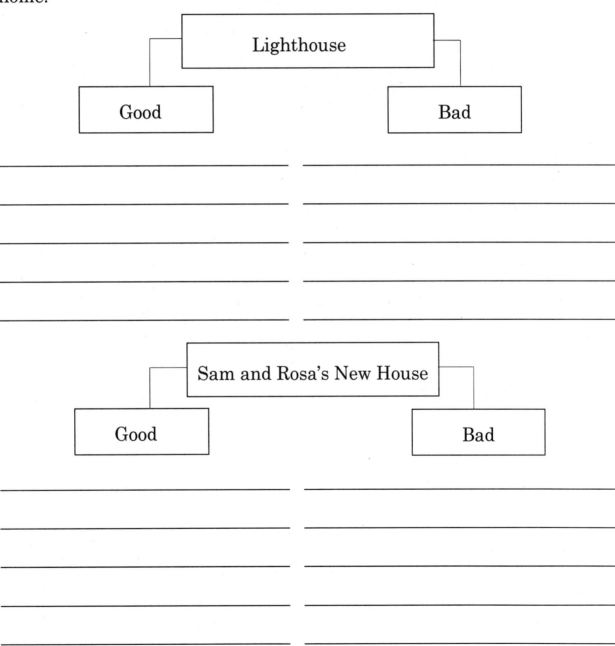

PAGES 26 - 32

Vocabulary: Use the words in the Word Box to fill in the crossword puzzle. Then use those words to fill in the blanks in the sentences below.

> **WORD BOX**
>
> sound   miss   found   spread   wings   flew

Across

1. moved through the air

4. something you hear

5. open out

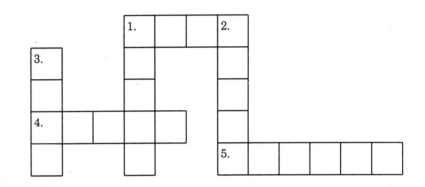

Down

1. got by looking

2. what a bird uses to fly

3. feel the loss of something

1. We will _____ you when you move away.

2. What is that loud _____ I hear?

3. I looked all morning before I _____ the key.

4. An eagle _____ over our house yesterday.

5. The sea gulls _____ their _____ and took off.

Pages 26 - 32 (cont.)

Read to find out how Sam and Rosa's wish comes true.

Story Questions:

1. Why does everyone run to Sam and Rosa's yard?

2. How do you know that Sam and Rosa really knew the sea gulls well?

3. Who are the "lighthouse children"?

4. Why do Sam and Rosa keep their light shining?

Picture Questions:

1. How do you know the neighbors are happy to see the birds?

2. How do you know this story takes place in a warm, sunny setting?

Questions for Discussion:

1. Why do you think Sam and Rosa call the sea gulls their "lighthouse children"?

2. Do you think this story could have really happened?

3. Do you know of any other stories in which animals travel a long way to be with people they like?

Pages 26 - 32 (cont.)

Cause and Effect:

Think about what happened in the story. Draw a line from *what happened* to *why it happened*.

What Happened	**Why It Happened**
1. A hundred sea gulls flew to the lighthouse every day.	a. There was a bad storm at sea.
2. The lighthouse had holes in the wall and no roof.	b. Sam and Rosa put up a light over their new house.
3. Sam and Rosa were never lonely in their new home.	c. The sea gulls loved the couple who fed them.
4. One day the sea gulls flew to Sam and Rosa's new house.	d. Sam and Rosa's neighbors invited them to parties and cookouts.

Writing Activity:

Pretend you are a newspaper reporter who lives in Sam and Rosa's neighborhood. Write a TV news story that tells how they helped their lighthouse children find them. Deliver your news story to the class.

CLOZE ACTIVITY

Read this story summary. Then go back and fill in each blank with a word that makes sense.

Sam and Rosa lived near the edge of the sea in a lighthouse.

At night they shone a _____[1] to guide the ships. Sam

_____[2] Rosa were not lonely because _____[3] gulls

flew in every day. _____[4] couple loved the birds and

_____[5] them food. One night the _____[6] started

to blow and giant _____[7] crashed down on the lighthouse.

_____[8] and Rosa could not fix _____[9] damage,

so they had to _____.[10]

Sam and Rosa found a new _____[11] far from the sea.

They _____[12] not lonely because they had _____[13]

neighbors. But the couple did _____[14] the birds.

One night Rosa _____[15] Sam shone a bright light

_____[16] their new house. They waited _____[17]

waited. One day the birds _____[18] to their yard. Sam, Rosa,

_____[19] their neighbors fed the sea _____[20]

and had a good time. Now the old couple keep the light shining from their

house to make sure the birds will return again.

POST-READING ACTIVITIES

1. Make a new cover for *The Lighthouse Children*. On the front, draw a picture that shows your favorite part of the book. On the back, write a few sentences that will make other people want to read the book.

2. Make a pair of sea gull hand puppets. Use a white sock for the body and attach cardboard wings and a beak.

3. Use cardboard and other materials to make a model of a lighthouse. Use a flashlight and mirror for the light.

4. Use modeling clay or paper-mache to create a sea gull or other bird that interests you. Paint the figure so the colors are true to life.

5. Find out five facts about sea gulls. Here are some questions to answer:

   - What do sea gulls eat?

   - Do they build nests?

   - How many eggs do they lay?

   - Do sea gulls fly south in winter?

   - Can they rest on the ocean?

   Make up some questions of your own.

6. Make up a story about a bird or groups of birds that come to visit you every day. Tell what you do to take care of them.

SUGGESTIONS FOR FURTHER READING

Bonsall, Crosby. *And I Mean It, Stanley*. HarperCollins.

* _____. *The Case of the Hungry Stranger*. HarperCollins.

_____. *The Day I Had to Play with My Sister*. HarperCollins.

\# Freeman, Don. *Corduroy*. Penguin.

_____. *Norman the Doorman*. Penguin.

* Hoban, Lillian. *Arthur's Camp-Out*. HarperCollins.

_____. *Joe and Betsy the Dinosaur*. HarperCollins.

_____. *Silly Tilly's Thanksgiving Dinner*. HarperCollins.

* Hurwitz, Johanna. *Rip-Roaring Russell*. Penguin.

Lobel, Arnold. *Days with Frog and Toad*. HarperCollins.

* _____. *Frog and Toad Are Friends*. HarperCollins.

* _____. *Frog and Toad Together*. HarperCollins.

_____. *Mouse Soup*. HarperCollins.

_____. *Uncle Elephant*. HarperCollins.

* Minarik, Else H. *Little Bear*. HarperCollins.

_____. *Little Bear's Friend*. HarperCollins.

Parrish, Peggy. *Dinosaur Time*. HarperCollins.

Some Other Books by Syd Hoff

Chester. HarperCollins.

* *Danny and the Dinosaur*. HarperCollins.

Mrs. Brice's Mice. HarperCollins.

Oliver. HarperCollins.

Sammy the Seal. Harper Collins.

Stanley. HarperCollins.

Who Will Be My Friend? HarperCollins.

* NOVEL-TIES Study Guides are available for these titles.

\# **Little Novel-Ties** Study Guide is available for this title.

ANSWER KEY

Pages 5 - 11

Vocabulary: 1. shone 2. careful 3. beam 4. hungry 5. guide 6. couple 7. lonely 8. lighthouse; *Answer:* sea gulls

Story Questions: 1. Lighthouses guide ships away from land and rocks. 2. Sam and Rosa aren't lonely because a hundred sea gulls come to visit them daily. 3. The sea gulls fly to the lighthouse because Sam and Rosa feed them. 4. It is clear that Sam and Rosa like the gulls because they photograph and paint them. 5. The birds fly away because gulls cannot stay in one place for very long.

Picture Questions: 1. Sam and Rosa's white hair show that they are old. 2. Sam and Rosa feed bread to the gulls. 3. Sam and Rosa carry bread to the gulls in paper bags.

Pages 12 - 17

Vocabulary: 1. storm 2. foghorn 3. damage 4. crashed 5. worry 6. tomorrow; 1. foghorn 2. tomorrow 3. storm 4. worry 5. crashed 6. damage

Story Questions: 1. Sam and Rosa don't worry when the sea gulls fly away because they know they will come back the next day. 2. Sam and Rosa keep ships safe by shining a beam of light and sounding the foghorn. 3. During the storm, waves crash into the lighthouse and do great damage. 4. After the storm, Sam and Rosa decided to move away to a new house.

Picture Questions: 1. The lantern that Rosa carries upstairs makes the light in the lighthouse tower. 2. The high waves and lightning show that it is a bad storm. 3. The lighthouse door is ripped off in the storm.

Pages 18 - 25

Vocabulary: 1. e 2. d 3. c 4. f 5. a 6. b; 1. waited 2. plain 3. neighbors 4. edge 5. cookout 6. visit

Story Questions: 1. Sam and Rosa move to a house far from the edge of the sea. 2. Sam and Rosa are not lonely because their new neighbors visit and invite them to parties and cookouts. 3. In their new home, Sam and Rosa miss the sea gulls from their lighthouse. 4. The gulls cannot visit because they do not know where Sam and Rosa live. 5. Sam and Rosa shine a beam of light from their new house to let the sea gulls know where they live. Answers to the second part of the question will vary.

Picture Questions: 1. Sam and Rosa travel in a pickup truck. 2. The neighbors serve hot dogs and hamburgers at the cookout. 3. Sam and Rosa decorate their house with Rosa's paintings of the sea gulls.

Pages 26 - 32

Vocabulary: Across — 1. flew 4. sound 5. spread; Down — 1. found 2. wings 3. miss; 1. miss 2. sound 3. found 4. flew 5. spread, wings

Story Questions: 1. Everyone runs to the yard when they hear the sound of wings. 2. Sam and Rosa called the birds by their names. 3. The sea gulls are the lighthouse children. 4. Sam and Rosa keep the light shining so the gulls will return.

Picture Questions: 1. You can tell that the neighbors are happy to see the birds because they smile and bring food for the birds to eat. 2. It is clear that this is a warm, sunny place because the grass is green, there are leaves on the trees, and the people go outside in lightweight clothing.